LEADING ADVISOR

VOL. 3

SPOTLIGHTS ON REMARKABLE
FINANCIAL PROFESSIONALS AND ADVISORS

LEADING ADVISOR

VOL. 3

SPOTLIGHTS ON REMARKABLE
FINANCIAL PROFESSIONALS AND ADVISORS

LEADING FINANCIAL
PROFESSIONALS AND ADVISORS

FEATURING:

Gregg Keele

Stephanie Campos

Tony Adamo

Matt A. Fassnacht

Julie Scates (Asti)

Curt Stowers

Thomas J. Diem

Teresa Yent

Nathan Brinkman

Remarkable Press™

Royalties from the retail sales of **"LEADING ADVISOR Vol. 3: SPOTLIGHTS ON REMARKABLE FINANCIAL PROFESSIONALS AND ADVISORS"** are donated to the Global Autism Project:

AUTISM KNOWS NO BORDERS; FORTUNATELY NEITHER DO WE.®

The Global Autism Project 501(C)3 is a nonprofit organization that provides training to local individuals in evidence-based practice for individuals with autism. The Global Autism Project believes that every child has the ability to learn, and their potential should not be limited by geographical bounds. The Global Autism Project seeks to eliminate the disparity in service provision seen around the world by providing high-quality training to individuals providing services in their local community. This training is made sustainable through regular training trips and contiguous remote training. You can learn more about the Global Autism Project and make direct donations by visiting **GlobalAutismProject.org.**

Leading Advisor Vol. 3/ Mark Imperial —1ˢᵗ ed

Managing Editor/ Shannon Buritz

ISBN: 978-1-954757-15-8

CONTENTS

A NOTE TO THE READER

Thank you for obtaining your copy of "LEADING ADVISOR Vol. 3: Spotlights on Remarkable Financial Professionals and Advisors." This book was originally created as a series of live interviews; that's why it reads like a series of conversations, rather than a traditional book that talks at you.

My team and I have personally invited these professionals to share their knowledge because they have demonstrated that they are true advocates for the success of their clients and have shown their great ability to educate the public on the topic of Financial Planning.

I wanted you to feel as though the participants and I are talking with you, much like a close friend or relative, and felt that creating the material this way would make it easier for you to grasp the topics and put them to use quickly, rather than wading through hundreds of pages.

So relax, grab a pen and paper, take notes, and get ready to learn some fascinating insights from our Leading Advisors.

Warmest regards,

Mark Imperial
Publisher, Author, and Radio Personality

INTRODUCTION

"LEADING ADVISOR Vol. 3: Spotlights on Remarkable Financial Professionals and Advisors" is a collaborative book series featuring leading professionals from across the country.

Remarkable Press™ would like to extend a heartfelt thank you to all participants who took the time to submit their chapter and offer their support in becoming ambassadors for this project.

100% of the royalties from this book's retail sales will be donated to the Global Autism Project. Should you want to make a direct donation, visit their website at GlobalAutismProject.org

GREGG KEELE

GREGG KEELE, CFP®, CRPC®, CDFA®

Conversation with Gregg Keele, CFP®, CRPC®, CDFA®

Gregg, you are a Certified Divorce Financial Analyst with Smarter Divorce Solutions, LLC. Tell us about your work and the people you help.

Gregg Keele: At Smarter Divorce Solutions, we help folks unwind bad marriages without destroying themselves, their families, their relationships with their children, and other important people in their lives. It's a tough time. People are often angry, and they want to fight or poke the other person as hard as they can. Our job is to help manage those emotions, the reality of the new situation, and find a way for both parties to go away feeling happy and satisfied. All it takes is a little bit of mutual respect and tact so that each relationship can be preserved as much as possible.

What are some common challenges your clients face?

Gregg Keele: Well, one of the difficulties of going through this process is that there's no shortage of folks in our lives who want to give us divorce advice. And most of that advice is pretty bad. I advise people to find a qualified and trusted, certified divorce financial analyst to help assess their financial situation and ease some of their worries. We work with many high net worth families, where one spouse hasn't worked in a long time or gave up their career for other endeavors, such as raising children or working with charities. Depending on the state you live in, breaking that up can be very stressful. So it really starts with sitting down and understanding what the marital assets are and what expectations need to be reset to exit the marriage. It's a tough time because usually there's some trauma; someone cheated, someone lied, someone did something offensive, or any combination of those. But we usually find that no good marriage ends in divorce. So usually, these are symptoms of a relationship that probably should have ended a long time ago anyway. And it allows everybody to move on to a better situation and a happier life. It's just getting from the point of having a lot of fear and anger to the point of acceptance and optimism about living a happier life.

What pillars guide you through the process while evaluating different divorce situations?

Gregg Keele: We work with folks in various situations: co-operative, collaborative, litigated, complicated, messy, loving, fighting. In a case where one person is financially disadvantaged, we look at how to reorder that person's life in the short term, midterm, and long term. Perhaps they will need some extra liquidity from the marital estate for the first three or four years just to get back on their feet or start to work again. If working isn't necessary, they may need help to reorient living and shopping habits to the reality of splitting the marital estate in half. Living off half, you have to reevaluate expectations and values about what is important. It is essential to understand the assets and who benefits most from each one based on their tax rate and liquidity of the asset. Some things might not pay off for a few years, which would not be helpful to a person who needs money right now. A person with a lot of income may benefit more from low tax basis assets, while someone with low income may be able to take tax-deferred assets and even out the estate that way. That is where we can provide a significant advantage to our clients.

Attorneys are often expertly trained in the law and have very little or no formal training in finance. So when you get into some of these assets, even something as simple as a 401K, many folks not trained in finance wouldn't know that the employer stock inside the 401K may qualify for special tax treatment. They may not be familiar with the particular laws of a 401K around divorce and how they differ from an IRA. There are three kinds of 457 plans. They're all named a 457B plan, but they all have different implications in divorce. I talked to an attorney the other day who was looking at some non-qualified stock options, and the market price was below the option price. She said, "Well, they're worthless, right?" Well, they had seven or eight years until expiration. So under Black-Scholes modeling, they were absolutely not worthless. But the attorney would have made that mistake and counted those assets as zero had she not reached out to me. So these are the things we look at. How do we get more out of each settlement than meets the naked eye?

Does it make things easier if the divorcing parties are financially equal?

Gregg Keele: Well, in some ways, it does make it easier because there's less fear on each side about being poor and not able to make it. Or if the children are still minors, not being able to take care of the kids or keep them in the same school district. So when both parties are relatively healthy in their earnings, they can take care of themselves, if you will. It does make the process of splitting the assets less stressful. I don't know if it's easier, but it's undoubtedly less stress on that end of the ledger, which allows us sometimes to have more productive conversations faster.

Gregg, what inspired you to get started in the financial services field?

Gregg Keele: I, unfortunately, went through a divorce seven or eight years ago that was not my choice. It was a really painful exercise. In fact, I did a combat tour in Iraq with the Army a few years before that. And I would do that several more times before I'll do one more divorce. But my ex-wife is a lovely person. And as much as we wanted to fight and hate each other and destroy everything, we were able to find something deep inside that could resist the insatiable desire to fight and hate and hurt. And we were able to eat some poop sandwiches and let things go.

As a result, to this day, she and I are friends. We co-parent well, and we decided to live a mile apart so that it wouldn't affect our children. And we've been able to focus consistently on not how it affects me or how it affects you, but instead this one chance at childhood that our kids get. We're not going to screw that up any more than we have to. We stay focused on coming out of this as better people and ultimately creating better experiences for the children because we are no longer in a bad marriage and happier. Our children are happy and successful. I think they'll tell us when they're 30, which is a ways away, that they didn't have much stress due to our divorce. I bring that perspective to the work I do. I help other families get to this place where all of their lives are better because they could end a bad relationship with personal courage and grace. That's just great work to put into the universe. So that's why I do it.

How has the recent pandemic impacted your industry?

Gregg Keele: It has changed perspectives considerably. In fact, during the pandemic, we saw divorces drop dramatically. And there were a lot of theories that out of the pandemic, we would have a baby boom and a divorce boom. Interestingly enough, the birth rate also dropped as people were unwilling to expose themselves or their babies to the risk of pregnancy during that time, which is very rational. But also, the same thing happened on the divorce side. People didn't want to be going through a divorce and either have to live together or live isolated somewhere else for an unforeseeable amount of time. And now we're starting to see that open up again. Perspectives have changed, and we're getting a flood of new divorces as restrictions ease from the government and other places. There has been a greater focus on the fact that life is short, and living another day, week, or month in misery isn't acceptable. We need to live each moment of this precious life while giving our greatest gifts with as much love and happiness as we can. And if you're in a bad relationship that's not working, you need to fix it or end it. We've all noticed in ourselves and the people around us that the last couple of years have had quite an emotional impact. And I know we've felt it, and we've let it slide through. But I would encourage everyone to take a little time, whether alone or with a religious leader or therapist, to just feel through some of the impact of the last two years and find some healing.

How can people find you, connect with you, and learn more?

Gregg Keele: My website is www.smarterdivorcesolutions. com/indiana. You can also reach me by phone at (317) 526-9869 so that we can determine if what I do aligns with your needs.

GREGG KEELE, CFP®, CRPC®, CDFA®

Certified Divorce Financial Analyst

Smarter Divorce Solutions, LLC

Gregg is a Certified Divorce Financial Analyst at Smarter Divorce Solutions, LLC. Gregg has Bachelor's degrees in both Economics and Political Science. He has earned the Certified Financial Planner (CFP®), Chartered Retirement Planning Counselor (CRPC®), Certified Divorce Financial Analyst (CDFA™), and Certification for Long Term Care (CLTC®) designations. Gregg served proudly as a Captain in the United States Army and did a combat tour in Iraq. He has over 24 years of experience as a financial advisor, has earned numerous awards and honors, and leads a team of twenty-two advisors and staff. Gregg's firm specializes in helping people recover from the trauma of divorce through compassionate, sustainable financial planning and litigation support. Additionally, his firm provides advisory services focused on executive compensation, estate, and retirement planning.

EMAIL: Gregg@SmarterDivorceSolutions.com

PHONE: (317) 526-9869

WEBSITE: www.smarterdivorcesolutions.com/indiana

STEPHANIE
CAMPOS

STEPHANIE CAMPOS, CFP®

Conversation with Stephanie Campos, CFP®

Stephanie, you are the Founder of Campos Financial in Miami, Florida. Tell us about your work and the people you help.

Stephanie Campos: I'm a CERTIFIED FINANCIAL PLANNER™, which is different from your average investment advisor because I'm considered board-certified under the CFP Board. The CFP® certification carries a fiduciary responsibility, so my recommendations have to be the best for each client's situation. While I'm happy to help everyone, most of my clients fall into the "sandwich generation" because they are balancing taking care of young children and older family members at the same time.

What common concerns do people in the "sandwich generation" have?

Stephanie Campos: One of the main things we discuss is taking care of older family members who have been retired for a while and are living alone. Even if living independently isn't a problem yet, sometimes it makes sense to sell the family home to downsize or be closer to family. Usually, clients have experienced being a caretaker before or seen others they know take on that role. Long-term care planning can be anything from relocating into a retirement community, setting up someone to visit the home for a few hours a day to help cook and clean, or simply buying a long-term care insurance policy. Planning ahead for this phase of life takes out a lot of the anxiety about what to expect and avoids having to make a last-minute decision.

How has the recent pandemic affected your industry?

Stephanie Campos: During the early part of the pandemic, everyone worried about the older people in their lives, whether they were in nursing homes or living independently. It brought to the forefront concerns regarding estate planning and life insurance. Many of my clients had to homeschool their children while schools were closed as an added complication. Some of us did this while working from home ourselves. If you didn't have emergency savings going into the pandemic and you were one of the many Americans sent home from work without any notice, then you had to make many tough financial decisions to keep your household running. Even if you had a nest egg saved, it might not have been enough. I work with all my clients to maximize their savings and ensure their families are covered for unforeseen emergencies.

Are there myths and misconceptions that prevent people from getting their finances in order?

Stephanie Campos: Sometimes, clients feel that there is no way they can pay off their high-interest credit cards or student loans. Refinancing the debt to a lower interest rate will save money within their budget, even if it's still half of the original rate. That savings can be used to pay down the loan earlier or save toward another goal. I help my clients put together a budget and then a savings schedule. We say, "OK. There's $400 leftover. Let's take that $400 over the next year, start the emergency fund and pay down the debt." Once those goals are met, we continue to move forward toward the next goal. Many student loan interest rates from years ago were 6% or higher, and they can now be refinanced to as little as 2.5% to 3%. I love to see clients take advantage of that strategy before the rates increase.

What mistakes do you help clients avoid?

Stephanie Campos: Since I'm both a financial advisor and an investment advisor, clients get very excited to invest. I understand because I love investing myself, but when you jump into investments without first organizing your budget and paying down debt, you're setting yourself up for possible failure. It's not that investing isn't a good idea. It's a good idea for everyone, but it's not the first step you need to make towards a healthy financial household. The first step is understanding your bills, spending habits and creating an emergency savings. Once you are confident that you won't need the funds you are investing for at least five years or more; then you can start a diversified portfolio.

Stephanie, what inspired you to get started in the financial services field?

Stephanie Campos: I grew up watching my mother throughout her career in banking. She and my grandparents were very good shepherds of our family's finances. They taught me to buy savings bonds with birthday money as a way to practice saving towards a goal. As I worked my way through college, saving and investing became a passion, and I knew it was something I had to focus on in my own career.

What should people look for when choosing a financial advisor?

Stephanie Campos: When looking for an advisor, a Certified Financial Planner is the best way to go. A CFP®, like myself, is held to the fiduciary standard - and that's what you really want. CFP® professionals must disclose conflicts of interest, perform thorough analysis before making recommendations, and can not place trades that negatively affect their clients. This is why a large number of CFP® professionals work independently and charge a flat fee rather than being tied to any one company.

How can people find you, connect with you, and learn more?

Stephanie Campos: I'm based out of Miami, Florida, but I work with clients across the country. I am always available via phone at 305-874-7480 or via chat on my website: www.camposfinancial.com.

STEPHANIE CAMPOS, CFP®

Founder

Campos Financial

Since 2004, Stephanie has been giving simple-to-follow financial advice to clients across the United States. Being raised by a single mother in New England, Stephanie learned the value of money and the importance of family early on. After graduating from Salve Regina University in Newport, Rhode Island, Stephanie found herself, like many of her clients, in the "sandwich generation." She cared for her elderly family members as well as her own growing family. Stephanie is well versed in balancing both short-term and long-term financial goals in the midst of market uncertainty. After her tenure at the two biggest brokerage firms in America, where clients referred to her as their financial "teacher," she obtained the CERTIFIED FINANCIAL PLANNER™ designation and established Campos Financial. Now, as an independent registered investment advisor, she enjoys helping clients manage and invest their finances so they feel confident in their own family's future.

WEBSITE: www.camposfinancial.com

PHONE: 305-874-7480

TONY
ADAMO

TONY ADAMO, AIF®

Conversation with Tony Adamo, AIF®

Tony, you are the co-founder of Wealth Advisors Who Care. Tell us about your work and the people you help.

Tony Adamo: I have been helping people retire successfully for 32 years. I co-founded our firm, Wealth Advisors Who Care, in 2018. We live our firm's name every day - we care about our Clients, the Community we live in and serve, and our planet's Climate. Our target market consists of small business owners, people within 5 to 10 years of retirement looking for some guidance on retiring, or already retired individuals. The recent pandemic shook people to their core. They realized they needed someone like myself, who is not only a Wealth Advisor but an Accredited Investment Fiduciary, who puts the client's interest before my own.

How has the pandemic impacted the financial services industry?

Tony Adamo: Since the financial crisis of 2009 and before the pandemic, the market has done extraordinarily well. We've had some corrections, but we really haven't had a crash. But in March of 2020, we saw the stock market go down about 30 to 40% within three weeks. Many people had not experienced anything like that. I started in this industry in October of 1987, which was infamous for the Black Monday crash, where the market went down 22% in one day. So 30% in 3 weeks when you haven't experienced that really shakes people up. People have reached out to us, realizing they might not know what they are doing and could use professional help. We stress there are two phases of retirement: the accumulation phase (where you are saving money) and the distribution phase (where you need to generate income from your assets). The analogy I use is climbing a mountain, where the top of the mountain is Retirement. The strategy for getting to the top of the mountain (Accumulation) and your strategy for descending the mountain (Distribution) are different. Some problems you might face in the Distribution Phase can include: Funds running short because of longevity, Health concerns causing unexpected costs, Volatility and Inflation in the market, Rising health care costs, and Estate taxes and end-of-life costs. People are typically looking for answers to these two questions: Can I retire when I want to? How do I generate a paycheck once I retire? How do I replace my salary with money coming out of my assets and additional sources of income other than Social Security? The value we provide our clients is twofold. One, we offer them clarity about where they are at today. More importantly, we provide them with a blueprint for getting through retirement successfully.

Are there common myths or misconceptions people have about managing their finances?

Tony Adamo: People think they can do it themselves. And don't get me wrong, what I do as a profession *can* be done by an individual, but it takes time and experience to become good at it. Especially now with the internet, there are self-directed accounts, low trading costs, and plenty of information. For instance, we're independent advisors, so we use Charles Schwab, Fidelity, and other institutions to custody the assets for our clients, and they provide tremendous educational information. So if you have the time, you can do it yourself. But I always ask, "Is that what you want to do in retirement?" Who wants to spend time looking at the market every day making adjustments? Do you really want to be focused on what's going on in the economy, interest rates, etc.? Or do you want to spend your retirement traveling and enjoying your family? I've had finance professors who thought that's what they wanted to do in retirement. But they ended up saying, " No, that's not what I want. I did this my entire life. You know, I'll hire somebody like yourself, who I trust, to do it so I can spend my retirement doing what I want to do."

Besides actually managing money, we are financial planners. We don't just evaluate their investments. I always tell clients, "You can have all the money in the world. But the number one thing you need to take care of is your health." And I give the great example of the late Steve Jobs. He was a very wealthy man, but all the wealth in the world could not stop his health from deteriorating. So we look at everything from fiscal to physical. And we plan for the "what ifs" in life. What if you become incapacitated? Who will handle your finances? What if you prematurely pass away? Do you have things in place to make sure family members or charities receive your assets? I consider myself a financial life manager.

What mistakes do you help people avoid?

Tony Adamo: Many people wait too long to plan for their retirement. I always tell clients, "The best day to plan for retirement was either yesterday or today." Don't procrastinate because planning sooner dramatically increases the probability of success. If you wait six months before you want to retire and then realize you can't, you are either going to have to work longer or drastically reduce your lifestyle. But if you plan within ten years and you're not on track, you can do things such as saving money and cutting expenses. You will have time to make adjustments.

The second big mistake is people thinking that 100% of their money needs to be in the stock market to retire successfully.

But that's not the case. That's not the case at all. The correct amount in stocks depends on your personal appetite for volatility or risk. We determine this by having a client complete a Risk Tolerance Questionnaire. We spend a lot of time at the beginning of the relationship to find out what is important to you and what you would like to do in retirement. The last thing we talk about is investments. In doing this for so long, I've realized that people will not make small changes. They will procrastinate and kick it down the road. But if you identify areas of their life that will be negatively impacted if they don't make a change regarding estate planning and incapacity, they *will* make the change. They realize we look at things from a different perspective. Most people sit down with a financial advisor and expect to talk about investments first. That's the last thing we talk about because if you don't have everything else squared away, the money won't matter. You need to have the proper protections in place for your family in the event of incapacitation or death.

Tony, what inspired you to get started in the financial services field?

Tony Adamo: It's a long story, but I'll give you the abridged version. When I was 22 years old, I was in the U.S. Army as a second lieutenant, and I got sent a direct mailer for a free steak dinner. I was single at the time and said, "Hey, I'll take the free steak dinner, and maybe I will even learn something."

And I did. I started investing at 22 years old, systematically every month, and I saw my money grow. That was before the crash of 1987. So when I transitioned from the military and a previous civilian career, I was looking for something that I enjoyed doing. I often tell people if I were not an advisor, I'd probably be a teacher because I love to educate people. I pride myself on client education. So when I decided to change careers, I looked for things that I enjoyed doing. In about a decade, I saw my money grow substantially. That is when I knew I wanted a career as a Financial Advisor.

What should people look for when choosing a financial advisor?

Tony Adamo: In our industry, there are great people, but some not-so-great people who take advantage of clients. First of all, find out what their credentials are. Are they a fiduciary, like myself? Are they a certified financial planner? There are many different designations. Get somebody that establishes your relationship with a financial plan, first and foremost. If they are only concerned about your investments, you should turn around and walk the other way.

Secondly, find out how long they've been working in the field. I always tell clients that if your advisor started in this industry after April 2009, it wasn't until March of 2020 that they actually experienced a crash in the market. You need someone who has experience with volatility, and more importantly, someone who can get you through it. A lot of our job is about psychology or behavioral finance and helping our clients manage the emotions of investing to help them achieve their long-term goals.

Why should a prospective client work with your firm?

Tony Adamo: Our firm was founded on the values of Objectivity, Integrity, & Fiduciary. Planning is powerful, but partnerships are paramount. Rather than following the sales-driven demands of a corporate office, we report to one person alone: to you, our client. Serving in a Fiduciary capacity, we remain transparent and objective in every way: from fees and costs to investment selections, financial strategies, and in every aspect of our business. By emphasizing process before products, our client-driven focus enables us to pursue your goals as if they were our own.

Integrity empowers us to provide truly objective advice and build solutions optimized for your success. While financial products may come and go, trusted relationships and custom solutions will stay the course. That's why we create comprehensive and flexible financial strategies that meet the needs of today while laying the foundation for tomorrow. We believe your goals, business commitments, and family situation deserve unique solutions that are customized to you and adaptable to change. When your life evolves, so should your strategies.

As a team, we will walk beside you through all stages of life's journey. Whether celebrating successes or navigating uncertain markets, we will work diligently to help you avoid emotional mistakes and stay on the path to financial freedom.

How can people find you, connect with you, and learn more?

Tony Adamo: Our website is www.wealthadvisorswhocare. com. You can also reach us by phone at 727-230-3800. I'm the company's co-founder, and my business partner's name is Chris Ritacca.

TONY ADAMO, AIF®

Co-Founder

Wealth Advisors Who Care

Throughout his life and career, Tony Adamo has always put the needs of others first. A Former US Army Artillery Officer and Captain, he has spent the last 32 years advancing the financial security of individuals, families, and business owners. While he thrives in a vast array of financial disciplines, he specializes in helping families manage a financial plan that incorporates investment risk management, retirement and income planning, legacy planning, incapacity planning, and more.

Partnering with his business colleague and longtime friend, Christopher Ritacca, Tony helped found Wealth Advisors Who Care in 2018. As Partner and Wealth Management Advisor, he draws on his years of experience working at leading firms, including TIAA, Charles Schwab, Fidelity, Dreyfus, Fifth Third Securities, and others. While utilizing his institutional experience and perspective, he delivers the personalized attention and service only a boutique firm can provide.

Tony first started investing at the young age of 22, then a 2nd Lieutenant in the US Army. He quickly experienced the value of watching his money grow by applying the principles of dollar-cost-averaging. From his first moment in the market to today, he has been committed to providing people with the guidance to grow their wealth and confidently pursue their financial goals.

Tony earned his Bachelor of Business Administration from Hofstra University and currently holds his Series 63 & 66 securities registrations, along with his Life, Health & Variable Annuity insurance licenses.

Tony earned the Accredited Investment Fiduciary® (AIF®) designation from the Center for Fiduciary Studies®, the standards-setting body for Fi360. The AIF designation signifies specialized knowledge of fiduciary responsibility and the ability to implement policies and procedures that meet a defined standard of care. The designation is the culmination of a rigorous training program, which includes a comprehensive, closed-book final examination under the supervision of a proctor and agreement to abide by the Center's Code of Ethics and Conduct Standards. On an ongoing basis, completion of continuing education and adherence to the Code of Ethics and Conduct Standards are required to maintain the AIF designation.

Originally from New York, Tony currently lives in Palm Harbor, Florida, with his wife, Debra Adamo. They enjoy their blended family of seven adult children & granddaughter. Actively involved in the community and charitable organizations, Tony is a former advocate for Big Brothers Big Sisters and a past member of the Palm Harbor Chamber of Commerce. A sponsor of the Tampa Chapter of "Heroes on The Water" & Mote Marine Lab. Member of the Military Officers of America Association (MOAA)

Outside of the office, he looks forward to golfing, traveling, and spending time with his family.

EMAIL: tadamo@wealthadvisorswhocare.com

PHONE: 727-230-3800

WEBSITE: www.wealthadvisorswhocare.com

LINKEDIN: https://www.linkedin.com/in/tony-adamo-aif%C2%AE-04503a13/

FACEBOOK: https://www.facebook.com/WealthAdvisorsWhoCare

TWITTER: https://twitter.com/WAWC2018

MATT A.
FASSNACHT

MATT A. FASSNACHT

Conversation with Matt A. Fassnacht

Matt, you are the co-founder of Meridian Investment Partners. Tell us about your work and the people you help.

Matt A. Fassnacht: I primarily do holistic financial planning for a wide variety of clients. Most of my clients are modern everyday working people with young families or people looking to retire within five to ten years. I work with business owners, as large IT firms are abundant in our area. In addition, many of my clients are executives for local businesses around Atlanta. Since my wife is from Shanghai, I have the opportunity to serve a global client base in the Greater Mainland China area. Because Atlanta is such a diverse transient city, my clients reside all around the world.

What common concerns do your clients have?

Matt A. Fassnacht: The most common concern across all cultures is people want to provide for their children, have money for their education, prepare them for life, to maximize their human potential. They are looking to accumulate and protect assets from any risk and put them in some kind of vehicle that will grow and be there for the future regardless of risks they cannot control.

How has the recent pandemic impacted the financial services industry?

Matt A. Fassnacht: The pandemic has changed a lot of things. From a technology perspective, face-to-face has become less common for many people. Zoom calls are certainly playing a more significant role in our day-to-day work. From a psychology perspective, the retiree generation has always been in a "accumulate and save" mindset. But the imminent mortality risk has caused people to say, "Hey, I can't take this money with me. I might as well use it to do things to make myself and others happy while I'm in this world." They may be more inclined to buy a new house, renovate an existing one, or purchase a new car. The Federal Reserve easy money policy has encouraged people to borrow and to use their assets while they can, as opposed to the mindset coming out of the last recession of "work, work, work, save, save, save," because you never know when the next disaster will strike. So I would say that the biggest human psychology change that I have seen with my clients and observing the world is the greater desire for freedom to enjoy life in whatever way you desire.

Are there any myths or misconceptions that prevent people from getting their finances in order?

Matt A. Fassnacht: The biggest thing is procrastination. We all fall into the trap of being comfortable with our own situation and what we're doing. We might not listen to other perspectives, think about different ideas, or talk to other people. In general, people want to keep it private when it comes to finances. I have also fallen into this trap, but I always learn new things from going to seminars and listening to people talk about ideas that I never even considered. As long as something has worked for people for a certain amount of time, it can be hard to fight that inertia and get them to want to make a change. But there can always be tweaks and improvements made to any situation.

Matt, what inspired you to get started in the financial services field?

Matt A. Fassnacht: In 2002, I was looking for help managing a partnership that involved financial advisors, attorneys, and several other professionals. From that experience, I learned that the field I am in has specific inherent conflicts that can put the advisor in a position where they can easily take advantage of the client, whether that is the intention or not. Many advisors work for major corporations where the corporation has shareholders who push down sales mandates to the advisor, which are not in the clients' best interest. The shareholders are only interested in their own profitability. So that motivated me to find a different way to operate in this industry, which is why I am set up as an independent financial advisor. Our goal at my firm will always be to do the best things for the client and put their interests first to help them achieve their financial goals in the most cost-efficient, effective way possible. We're not here to push products down people's throats that they do not need or want so that we can maximize our own profitability.

What should people look for when choosing a financial advisor?

Matt A. Fassnacht: Advisors set up as CFPs and who have a Chartered Financial Analyst qualification like myself are typically set up to be fiduciaries for our clients, meaning that we act in their best interest at all times. We put our clients ahead of ourselves. Always ask if the advisor you are considering working with is a fiduciary and independent of the specific custodian. People often worry about advisors "taking their money and using it for personal purposes" because of the whole Bernie Madoff situation. I work with various custodians, most notably Schwab and Fidelity, who custody the assets I manage on behalf of my clients. I do not have custody of client assets. My role is to make investment decisions on the client's behalf.

How can people find you, connect with you, and learn more?

Matt A. Fassnacht: My website is investmeridian.com, where you can find more information about me. I love to speak with people. So the best way is to call me at 404-585-5946.

MATT A. FASSNACHT

Co-Founder

Meridian Investment Partners

Matt Fassnacht is co-managing partner of Meridian Investment Partners, an Atlanta, GA-based Registered Investment Advisory Firm that specializes in wealth management to maximize clients' assets and reduce their risk so that they can make the most of life. Matt was born in Dunwoody, GA, and spent most of his formative years in Dunwoody, GA (a suburb north of Atlanta) and Upper St. Clair (a suburb south of Pittsburgh, PA). His first job was as a local neighborhood paperboy for the Pittsburgh Post-Gazette, and he became an avid Steelers fan. Matt graduated from Clemson University (99-02) with a B.S. in Accounting and played on the Clemson football team as a defensive player in the three years at Clemson. His professional career began in audit and tax for public accounting firms, and he obtained his CPA license in 2005. Matt later worked in corporate financial planning and analysis for Delta Airlines, guiding them through the Northwest Airlines merger integration and helping them turn around to lead the industry in profitably and customer satisfaction among the major US airlines. He went on to co-found Meridian Investment Partners in 2011. He became a CFA Charterholder from CFA institute in 2012. CFA Institute's mission is to lead the investment profession globally by promoting the highest standards of ethics, education, and professional excellence for the ultimate benefit of society. He lives in East Cobb and is married with two children. Matt's hobbies are aviation and gardening, as he enjoys nurturing his backyard orchard of various fruit trees and plants.

EMAIL: maf@investmeridian.com

PHONE: 404-991-8489

WEBSITE: www.investmeridian.com

JULIE SCATES (ASTI)

JULIE SCATES (ASTI), CFP

Conversation with Julie Scates (Asti), CFP

Julie, you are the founder of Asti Financial Management. Tell us about your work and the people you help.

Julie Scates (Asti): We do broad financial planning and investment management. The people that we work with are individuals, families, and small businesses. We work with what I like to call middle income, not ultra high net worth individuals, but just everyday folks that need financial planning help.

We help our clients plan for their future goals - planning for a secure retirement, funding children's educations, purchasing a home, etc. We also help people reach their short-term goals - funding a remodel, paying down debt, deciding to buy or lease a car, or making extra payments on their mortgage.

We also assist with the different financial decisions associated with those goals. For example, in looking at college planning, we help with funding decisions - saving to a 529 or another investment account, taking student loans, understanding if they qualify for financial aid or whether they should use home equity.

We are a little bit different than most firms in that we work much like a doctor or a lawyer on an hourly basis. So we don't do the traditional 1% assets under management, and we don't sell any products or earn any commissions. We act as a fiduciary for clients (always putting their best interests first) with a unique business model in the investment industry.

What common challenges do your clients face?

Julie Scates (Asti): There are two groups of people that we primarily work with. The first group is what I call accumulators. These are single people or couples who may have small kids and are trying to stretch their money to afford a new house or fund savings plans. If they have kids, they are trying to manage expensive daycare and childcare costs. They are also trying to save for their children's college educations and their own retirement. So their money is being pulled in many different directions. They come to us and say, "How do we manage all of this and attack our goals so that we reach them, even though we don't have unlimited funds to do everything we want to do?"

The second core group of people we work with are pre-retirees. It starts around age 50 when people realize retirement is coming up and say, "Let me do a check-in to find out what I can do to better prepare now. Do I need to save more? How can I ensure that I am doing all of the right things to have a solid future for myself?"

How has the recent pandemic impacted the financial services industry?

Julie Scates (Asti): In talking to friends and colleagues in my industry, all of our businesses have absolutely exploded. At the beginning of the pandemic, there were all of these jokes about people cleaning their baseboards and organizing their closets. Well, many of them also decided to get financially organized in the downtime they had as well. We have continued to be very busy for the past two years, as people are paying attention to their finances, making a plan, and preparing for the future.

Are there any myths or misconceptions that prevent people from getting their finances in order?

Julie Scates (Asti): In direct relation to the pandemic, we saw the market decline significantly as the pandemic started. In terms of myths and misconceptions, it was the classic "phone ringing off the hook" with people panicking about the market declining. So we got a lot of calls from people wanting to sell and move into cash. My job is to stay calm and help clients remain calm and not panic sell. We've been through this before; the market goes down, but it always comes back up. 2020 ended with the stock market up about 20%. This year didn't feel so great, but we've ended the year up 28%+. So the myth and the misconception is that when the market crashes and people panic, they sell at the wrong time, go into cash, and then don't know when to reinvest. Our job has been to keep people calm, keep them invested, and keep growing their savings for the future.

In 'normal' times, many people may think there is nothing they can do to get their finances in order - they don't earn enough or have too much debt. We have yet to work with a client that we could not help be better prepared and more financially stable. There are always things you can do to improve your financial situation.

One common misconception is that people feel like they have too much cash. This can certainly be an issue, depending on how much cash they actually have. But in a low-interest-rate environment like we have now and with the stock market volatility we are experiencing, sometimes it's OK to have funds in cash - that may be the best option depending on market conditions and their own situation.

What mistakes do you help your clients avoid?

Julie Scates (Asti): Mortgage rates have gotten to 30+ year historic lows, in the 2 or 3% range. So we still find people wanting to rush to pay down their mortgage. There is a high cost of living in the Bay Area, where we're located. So most of my middle-income clients are making six figures, and they're in a high tax bracket. And under current tax laws, mortgage interest is one of the things that you can still write off; it's not tethered, meaning you don't have that cap of $10,000 on property taxes/state/local taxes. You can write off your mortgage interest up to $750,000. Sometimes, high earners want to throw all of their money at debt. If you are earning 10 to 20% in your investment accounts, why would you pull money from there to pay down a 2% debt that is tax-efficient? People tend to be debt-averse, but a mortgage is kind of 'good debt,' so you should keep your money where it will grow, rather than paying down your mortgage, depending on your situation.

Another area we see a lot is when clients bend over backward to pay for their children's educations - sometimes sacrificing their own retirement. We have seen clients refinance their homes as they are nearing retirement to draw funds out to pay for college. Many clients let their children choose any college they wish, including very expensive private colleges that charge $80k/yr! They don't have honest discussions about what they can and can't afford. They don't encourage their children to use low-cost community colleges for their general education courses or consider state schools. We understand people want the best for their children and don't want them graduating with mountains of student debt. Still, they need to have honest conversations about the funds they have for college and what they can realistically afford - and other financially beneficial options.

Lastly, we help clients get out of debt. It happens to the best of us - all of a sudden, your credit card balances are high, and you have large monthly payments that feel never-ending. We help clients develop a plan to get debt paid off as quickly as possible and manage their high-cost debt using lower interest options. Then we work to help them set up savings plans and work on their budgets so it doesn't happen again.

Julie, what inspired you to get started in the financial services field?

Julie Scates (Asti): Well, I have always been in the financial industry. I started on what we call the "buy-side." I worked for institutional money managers, and I was a money manager myself. So that was my background. I began looking at personal financial planning about 15 to 20 years ago. Back then, the industry was changing from the broker commission model into "let's help people just manage their finances and their money. Let's help them PLAN." Then I found this unique business model that was just emerging - the hourly model. And I thought to myself, "If I went to a financial planner, why would I pay them 365 days of the year to watch my portfolio, when the reality is, they're maybe doing quarterly or semi-annual rebalancing?" So I set up my business and this practice to offer fair, honest financial planning to people on an hourly basis. You pay us when you need help. And when you don't, you're not paying us. Most portfolios don't need to be 'babysat' and monitored daily. You can check on your portfolio quarterly or semi-annually and just pay for analysis and advice when you need it. That way, we can help people with not only their investments but also their insurance, taxes, college planning, and other things that people are not equipped to deal with. I mean, the average consumer never goes through any financial training or is taught how to manage money. We weren't taught this in school. How can they be expected to know all of this?! So I wanted to set up this business to provide advice and professionalism to help people make decisions that nobody else has ever taught them how to make - in a cost-effective way.

Is there anything else you would like to share with our readers?

Julie Scates (Asti): Many people look at the cost of financial planning and don't really consider the benefits. But paying our fees can save you from making bad decisions and help ensure a secure future that you wouldn't have without professional help. It's like pennies on the dollar for the benefits you will receive. With our help, your portfolio could grow, and you could make better financial decisions that could make all the difference when it comes to you retiring securely, sending your kids off to college, and paying off your debt. People really have to think about the cost and the benefits.

How can people find you, connect with you, and learn more?

Julie Scates (Asti): The best way is our website at www.astifinancial.com. It's a great website because we are totally transparent. We have all of the information on what we do, how we do it and are very clear on our fees. There's a nice little button that you can click to schedule a call directly with my associates or me. We offer an introductory call to talk about your situation and see if it makes sense for us to continue to a meeting to talk further and in more detail about your situation and how we may be able to provide value. For project clients, this initial meeting is a planning session and is totally complimentary. For clients who want to work on an hourly only basis, our next step would be to set up a 2 hour paid advisory meeting.

JULIE SCATES (ASTI), CFP

Founder

Asti Financial Management

Asti Financial Management, LLC was founded over 15 years ago out of a desire to help individuals gain control over their finances and to maximize their wealth in order to realize their goals and dreams. We help people live a healthy, balanced life, trying to reduce the stress of worrying about their financial futures. Our firm has always been completely independent and not affiliated with any broker/dealer as we want to be 100% objective in any strategies or products recommended to clients. This business is built on our reputation, and we are a Fiduciary to our clients.

This is not just a business – it is an extension of personal values. We work to provide honest, high-quality, easy-to-understand, and implement financial planning advice to individuals, their families, and small businesses.

Julie brings clients over 30 years of experience in the financial services and investment management industry, having worked with small independent financial firms to very large organizations like Barclays Global Investors, creating and launching their iShares products.

Julie earned her Certified Financial Planner™ credential in 2006. She attended the University of California, Berkeley. She received a Graduate Certificate, with honors, in Personal Financial Planning (2005) and a Bachelor of Science in Finance, Banking, and Real Estate from San Francisco State University (1991).

Julie is currently serving on the Board of Directors for BFAFE - a non-profit organization providing financial education to inner-city high school students. She is also an active member of the Financial Planning Association of San Francisco, having served on the Board and as Chapter President.

She is a Bay Area native and enjoys spending time with family and friends, exploring the Bay Area in all its uniqueness. She likes spending time at the tiny house she built with her husband in Murphys, CA., as well as traveling around the U.S. and abroad, having visited over 30 different countries and most of the United States.

EMAIL: julie@astifinancial.com

PHONE: 510.525.8557

WEBSITE: www.astifinancial.com

CURT
STOWERS

CURT STOWERS, PhD, CFP®

Conversation with Curt Stowers, PhD, CFP®

Curt, you are the founder of F5 Financial. Tell us about your work and the people you help.

Curt Stowers: F5 stands for Faith, Family, Friends, Fitness, and Finance. It's a reflection of how we look at the financial planning process. We're a little bit different than many firms in that we take a more holistic approach, helping families find financial freedom so they can pursue personal significance. We work with many folks who may not be totally enamored with their day-to-day life and are looking to make a change, but they just don't know whether or not they can do it financially. Most of our clients are in their mid-40s and trying to figure out what they want to do. We help them understand where they're at financially, where they want to go, and help them make the appropriate changes to pursue what is important to them.

How does your approach to financial planning differ from the traditional approach?

Curt Stowers: Historically, the financial services industry has been sales-based from a compensation structure standpoint. Financial planners would try to get in your pocketbook without letting you know. We do what is known as "fee-only" planning. Whenever we talk to a family, we let them know up front exactly what the charge will be. If you look at the industry as a whole, it seems to be going in that direction. So there are many fee-only planners, but the segment is still small compared to the total number of planners.

Secondly, many firms talk predominantly about investments, beating the market, and the next hot stock. We say money is just a tool, and you can't beat the market. We say, "Hey, folks, let's make sure we capture the market returns. But let's not try to go chasing ghosts that don't exist. And let's use that set of assets you have to support what is important to you. Let's make a plan and look at the whole picture to achieve your goals." We take a comprehensive, holistic approach, rather than the stockbroker calling you and trying to sell you products. Since there is a lot more to life than money, we help our clients set goals beyond financial aspects as well.

Are there common myths and misconceptions that prevent people from getting their finances in order?

Curt Stowers: We see people trying to beat the market again and again. If you turn on the news, the press always tries to convince people that they can do it. Everyone is always talking about how to make a fast buck. I'm not saying it can't be done. I am 100% certain some people make millions or even tens of millions playing in the stock market. But for most folks, it is a myth that you will get rich by trying to time the market or picking the magic stock.

Also, many people either think they don't have enough money to start financial planning, or they will "get to it later." But it really can't wait. I'm going to get into the mathematics of it because I love math. The power of compounding is just incredible. There's a famous rule called the Rule of 72, which says if you take an interest return rate, let's say 8%, and you divide it into 72, you get nine. It tells us your money is going to double every nine years. So if you take someone who is 30 years old and wants to work until they're 66, that's 36 years, which is four doubles: 2,4,8,16. So that person will have 16 times as much money as they have right now. So if they had $10,000, that grows up to $160,000. The myth is that you have time to put it off. You don't have time because you can't afford to wait.

You can start with very little money. If you come to me and say, "Hey, Curt, I got a $10,000 bonus. What do you think I should do with it?" The first time I'll say, "Why don't you take half and go on vacation? All I need you to do is save the other half for me." You will probably go away feeling very happy as you get to go on vacation. Perhaps after that, you get a 10% raise. I'll say, "Take 5% and go on vacation and then save the other 5%." I've just played a little game with you here. The vacation is something that you don't have to do every year; it's something you *can* do. Next year, I will have 5% extra cash flow available to you when things come around! So I do this with families for a couple of years, saving half of each raise while they take the other half to do something from an experiential standpoint. A couple of years down the line, they've had the experiences, they're saving money, they've got more cash flow, and they are saying, "How is this happening?!" What I have done is keep them from expanding their lifestyle. Little tricks like this can make a big difference. Psychology is just as important as the quantitative aspect, so we strive to guide our clients with the right thought processes.

What mistakes do you help your clients avoid?

Curt Stowers: I'm a math and science guy, an engineer by background. So it's hard for me to relate to this. But the biggest thing I see is people coming to me and having no idea what they spend each month. So we can use some electronic tools such as YNAB or Quicken, hook up their bank accounts and credit cards, and track 6 to 12 months of transactions. Most people are shocked when they find out they spend $700 a month dining out. It's all about the subtle little things, and you have to be aware of the behavior.

Another thing I'll see is couples with separate bank accounts, and one person is carrying all of the debt, while the other has a bunch of excess cash. Why are you paying 18% interest over here when your partner has extra money? Why not pay it off? So those are probably two of the biggest mistakes I see my clients make.

Curt, what inspired you to get started in the financial services field?

Curt Stowers: That's an interesting question. I relocated to Chicago about a dozen years ago. I had an outstanding career with Caterpillar. At one point, I lived in the Middle East, and 600 people worked for me as I managed facilities in Brussels, Moscow, Manchester, and South Africa. It was just a wonderful experience. After I came to Chicago, I started working for a different part of the company. Within six months, my boss came into my office and said, "They're selling this part of the company, and the wall is going up. None of us can go back to Caterpillar." I had done well financially and had undergrad and graduate degrees in engineering. I was in a position to do what I wanted, and I certainly didn't like being told that I was being sold. It didn't sit well with me. So I started to think about what I was good at. Numbers and finance were things I had always enjoyed. I was a little too young to golf and fish all day. So I decided to make a change. I went through the process of researching how to become registered as a financial advisor and found out about the Certified Financial Planning Program and how to start my own business. I did that over a couple of years and slowly made the transition. I started my own firm in February of 2014. We started with zero clients and now have over 100 clients that we support, managing over $100 million in investments for their families.

What should people look for when choosing a financial advisor?

Curt Stowers: Google "how to find a financial advisor." If you do the research, you will quickly conclude that you want a fee-only advisor. The National Association of Personal Financial Advisors (NAPFA) website will provide you with an entire list. I would love the opportunity to talk to anyone looking for an advisor. But if you don't pick me, definitely choose one of the advisors you find on NAPFA. I just can't speak highly enough of the people in this field and the profession.

How can people find you, connect with you, and learn more?

Curt Stowers: Our website is www.f5fp.com. We have an extensive library of blog posts that are all self-created and information on a wide variety of topics. Take a look at all of our resources. If you decide to speak with me, there is a scheduling widget since we like our technology. Jump on my schedule, and I would be happy to talk with you, obligation-free. I speak to dozens of people I don't end up working with each year. I feel very blessed with how my life has played out. Every time I help someone who doesn't become a client, I speak with someone who does a week or two later. So I love to have discussions and see what we can do to get you on the right track.

CURT STOWERS, PhD, CFP®

Founder

F5 Financial

Curt Stowers is a Certified Financial Planner and founder and president of F5 Financial, a fee-only financial planning firm with offices in Naperville, IL, McDonough, GA, and Venice, FL, and serving clients nationwide (virtually).

Curt is a graduate from the University of Illinois, where he earned a BS, MS, and PhD in Industrial Engineering. He's a husband, father of three, an avid outdoorsman, and a follower of Christ.

Curt's goal as a financial planner is to ensure that families, corporate executives, and entrepreneurs have a comprehensive financial plan in place to reach their life goals. With 18 years of experience as a corporate executive and having owned a Subway franchise for over a decade, he knows how to provide practical, first-hand perspectives in the financial planning process.

At F5 Financial, Curt and his team take a holistic approach to financial planning, personal goals, and behavioral change. Using their F5 Process and Financial Health Cycle, they provide insight and tailored strategies that inspire and equip clients to enjoy a life of significance and financial freedom.

EMAIL: curt.stowers@f5fp.com

PHONE: (630) 474-5213

WEBSITE: https://www.f5fp.com/

LINKEDIN: https://www.linkedin.com/in/curtstowers

FACEBOOK: https://www.facebook.com/curt.stowers

THOMAS J. DIEM

THOMAS J. DIEM, CFP®, ChFC®

Conversation with Thomas J. Diem, CFP®, ChFC®

Thomas, you are the founder of Diem Wealth Management. Tell us about your work and the people you help.

Thomas Diem: We help people retire right. Most of our new clients are within five years of retirement or have retired in the last five years and would like to make some adjustments. Hiring a qualified advisor could be a beneficial adjustment. What we do is to help people better understand their own financial situation. We show them the challenges they face and how they can reduce costs and then increase efficiency through the elimination of unrewarded risks and costs within their current portfolio. Monitoring the progress and updating the plan is a large part of our collaboration with the client. If a portfolio becomes unbalanced over time, the risk level will often rise and could become above the client's comfort level.

Diem Wealth is a Fiduciary. We operate under the Fiduciary Standard set forth by the Certified Financial Planner Board of Standards. As a CFP° professional, we must describe to the Client the qualitative and quantitative information concerning the Client's personal and financial circumstances needed to fulfill the Scope of Engagement and collaborate with the Client to obtain necessary information.

We help the Client identify, select and prioritize their goals.

We analyze the Client's current course of action and help them better understand alternative courses of action.

We assist the Client in implementing the plan. Fees and any potential conflicts are disclosed. Risks the client could face are clearly communicated to the client.

Monitoring our Client's progress and identifying updates to the plan is an ongoing service.

What common challenges do your clients face?

Thomas Diem: Many people tend to have a junk drawer full of investments, insurance, wills, trusts. They just aren't very well organized, and therefore, their thought is not very well organized. Most people don't understand basic investment theory, so it often feels like information overload. It's usually not taught in school. They go out into this financial wilderness initially through the internet. They may attend a seminar, read a book, or watch some YouTube videos. After this overload, many instinctively think a money manager might be able to help them out. In many cases, that's absolutely not true. Working with a CFP* professional can demystify the noise, sales-oriented approaches and replace that with a competent, simple-to-understand framework along with continuing, custom-tailored advice.

What mistakes do you help your clients avoid?

Thomas Diem: Many people are not paring down their risk as they approach retirement. They have watched their 401k statements go up, and then suddenly, something goes wrong. Then they find themselves having too much risk and too much downside. A quick market downturn in a few months could cause them to retire years later than they initially hoped. This is usually the result of not having a complete financial plan from beginning to end. In our income analysis, we marshal together all the sources of income, and then we get a realistic expectation of their retirement expenses. The effects of inflation and expected market volatility are factored into this work. Many people underestimate these living expenses after their working years. We see this all the time when people are earning quite a bit of money, and then all of a sudden, they retire and find that their budget ideas are a small percentage of what they will really need for retirement. So they tend to overestimate their ability to retire comfortably. We help provide a cushion, a safety net, through our communication with the clients. Managing client expectations is a big part of what we do and goes a long way toward a relationship without unfortunate surprises. Many pre-retirees have done a fine job of saving and growing their money before retirement. We help bring people into their new retirement home in a way they can enjoy it.

How has the pandemic impacted the financial services industry?

Thomas Diem: The pandemic has not changed the actual investment or retirement processes. It has only changed the way we communicate. We do more screen shares, Zoom meetings, and phone conversations. We're okay with people not coming into the office, as we have many ways to communicate with them. It has been nice to see things opening up in Fort Wayne. We just reopened our retirement seminars with packed houses at these events. The attendance is expected to be high at our upcoming events as well.

Thomas, what inspired you to get started in the financial services field?

Thomas Diem: I have always been in finance. I guess I never had a real job. My mom and I were working with a broker at a large national firm, which was my initial source of inspiration. We were paying all of this money to have this person help us, and I thought, "This can be done much better." So I became a stockbroker in a small boutique firm, which was a tough job but really helped me better understand the industry's inner workings. Over time, I evolved into this situation I'm now enjoying. I kept trying to improve, rebuild, and reimagine myself. I earned the certifications of CFP® and ChFC® and now help people develop and execute organized financial plans. As a Fiduciary, clients are more comfortable with our work, and it makes my life better by putting the client's interests ahead of the firm and myself. This has been the most important long-term professional goal I have achieved.

What should people look for when choosing a financial advisor?

Thomas Diem: The usual response is to only deal with someone you can trust. This, of course, is a given. But how does one know who to trust? My advice is to become a little better educated on personal finance. It is not as difficult as people in the industry would have you believe. Through our website and social media platforms, we provide an abundance of educational material designed to help people better understand the challenges they face in today's financial jungle. We have worked hard not to be a part of all the noise and provide concise, easy-to-understand information. I would like to think there are good people helping their clients in all types of business settings, but the firms supporting these professionals have made things difficult. We've worked very hard to eliminate the middleman and complete a direct pipeline from the consumer to the products and services they need. That is a highly unlikely probability to accomplish with broker-dealer firms. Many banks, insurance firms, and financial networks also have platform fees that primarily support profit centers within the firm. You have to find out exactly what these costs are because fees matter. I often have new clients come to me and say, "I don't really care what you charge, as long as you make me money." But I tell them they need to know every detail about their costs. Both explicit and implicit fees come out of the investor's top line. So when you select someone to work with, make sure fees are discussed upfront because they can be easily hidden. Implicit trading costs on mutual funds are not disclosed in part A of the prospectus. Explicit total operating expense listed in the main prospectus or sales fact sheets is often less than total expense paid by the investor. We help people better understand how much they are paying with our fee analysis. Almost all people coming into our offices who have had this work done have been surprised or shocked at what they were paying.

Also, when people purchase fixed annuities, advisors often mistakenly tell them that the commission is paid on their behalf by the insurance company. This notion is akin to fairy dust. In every large city, there are large insurance company buildings built by internal costs of insurance products. No insurance company has ever paid a commission to an insurance agent without taking these costs from the person purchasing the annuity. There's a spread inside these fixed annuity products, which comes right out of the interest rate the contract owner would receive compared to a no-load product. One could gather that owners of these products are probably losing a point or more a year. There are also surrender charges assessed for getting out of the contract early. This helps the company recoup the commissions paid to the agent and the company marketing the product. But many advisors tell you that this is part of the overall plan, and there are no charges. So when dealing with a fixed annuity, always ask the advisor what their commission is on the product. If they're getting 7% commission on a 10-year annuity, you know that you're paying seven-tenths of a percent a year for just agent commissions. And then there's an additional cost for marketing companies on top of that. These are the companies that supply the insurance agent with products. So in total, it's probably an additional 1% a year or more each year just for sales and marketing. Don't forget about the costs associated with those big buildings filled with well-paid employees. Disclosure of these costs is not required by the SEC or the insurance company, but this can be roughly calculated. Most people have no idea what they are paying yet believe strongly they know their costs.

Also, ask the advisor what your level of risk is in terms of standard deviation. The standard deviation of your portfolio is the most important number to know the level of risk you are being advised to take on. This is a measure you can use to estimate your maximum reasonable downside of your portfolio. If you don't know this number or the advisor is only able to provide an ambiguous description of risk as moderate or conservative, you should move on to another advisor. A competent advisor can help you understand this number and how it could affect your retirement.

How can people find you, connect with you, and learn more?

Thomas Diem: Like us on Facebook at Diem Wealth Management. Our websites are www.tomdiem.com and www.diemwealth.com. A quick Google search of my name or the firm name will lead you to us as well. Our phone number is 260-918-8800. Setting an appointment for a no-cost, no-obligation review is recommended. This way, you get to meet us, learn some things about your own situation, and leave with some ideas that can save you some money.

THOMAS J. DIEM, CFP®, ChFC®

Founder

Diem Wealth Management

If not conducting a meeting, teaching a class, or flying to a speaking engagement, Tom can most likely be found in his offices in Fort Wayne, Indiana. Here you will often find him reading up on the latest tax law change, economic modeling technique, devouring the intricacies of an estate plan, or skillfully determining the best strategy to create a more fluid and effective financial model for someone.

This devoted Christian and family man is a health nut. If he isn't reading on how to better himself, he's on his road bike, doing laps at the pool, or just taking a long walk. Occasionally, he'll brave the depths for scuba diving or paddle for miles on a stand-up paddleboard. In 2020, during the pandemic, Tom became a student of electric guitar and performs in the band, Bucketlist. Bucketlist plays at medium-sized public stage venues.

Tom served three years in the U.S. Army, trained in Military Intelligence, and was stationed in Frankfurt, Germany.

Tom is a Certified Financial Planner™ and Chartered Financial Consultant® professional.

He started his financial career as an insurance agent and sales manager. Tom rose to a national leading sales manager and one of the youngest branch sales managers in company history with a leading insurance company. After working with financial advisors on his own portfolio, Tom became aware of the need for competent financial advice. This experience compelled Tom to become a financial advisor for a New York Stock Exchange member firm. He has been an independent advisor for the last twenty years. He has over 25 years of experience serving the needs of affluent and high-net-worth financial clients.

Please feel free to contact him for a no-obligation appointment to review your current situation and "Experience the Coaching Difference."

EMAIL: tom@diemwealth.com

PHONE: 260-918-8800

WEBSITE: www.diemwealth.com

FACEBOOK: https://www.facebook.com/diemwealth

TERESA YENT

TERESA YENT, ChFC, CLTC

Conversation with Teresa Yent, ChFC, CLTC

Teresa, you are the founder of Golden Years Advisors. Tell us about your work and the people you help.

Teresa Yent: We focus on the distribution phase of people's financial lives. Of course, we can help in the accumulation phase. But we specifically help people who are 5 to 10 years from retirement, and we do financial planning to distribute their accumulated wealth throughout their lives. Our goal is for them to spend confidently during the go-go years of retirement, knowing that the slow-go years and the no-go years are taken care of no matter what life has in store for them.

What challenges and fears do your clients face?

Teresa Yent: People are always fearful of running out of money during retirement. That's the number one fear. We do a tremendous amount of planning with cash flow. Once we have a plan in place, which is dynamic, ever-changing, and never stagnant, we have them bring us a list of their fears and their dreams. We have systems and software that allow us to stress-test their plan with their specific fears and dreams. We continue to work on their cash flow, fears, and dreams until the client is confident with their plan. If they aren't confident, it doesn't really matter if I think it's okay. The client has to be confident to truly enjoy their go-go years of retirement.

Long-term care is another fear that has come to light, especially during the pandemic. People are worried about being a burden on their children. So healthcare is a huge concern. Sometimes healthcare is a more significant concern than the money itself, simply because of the fear that surrounds it. Medical science is extending our lives, but it also creates more need for long-term care.

Is there confusion surrounding the topic of healthcare?

Teresa Yent: Many of our clients who are approaching 65 don't understand how Medicare works. The media scares them, and sometimes I wish my clients would just turn off the TV. The media doesn't say nice things about Medicare. Medicare is wonderful insurance, and it works very well. It might be a financial burden upon the United States and its treasury, but the way it works is fantastic for the patient. About six months prior to our client's 65th birthday, we do a session called "Medicare 101." We help clients choose a Medicare supplement, and every year during the annual enrollment period, we assist them with their Medicare Part D options. We also insist that you have to have a long-term care plan. That doesn't necessarily mean it has to be long-term care insurance; we just have to have a plan, which can be self-insuring. Most of our clients do what we call asset-based long-term care, which is a life insurance chassis that takes care of long-term care needs. If they don't ever use the policy, it has a death benefit, and their heirs get the proceeds. A lot of people really like that. This type of policy is better suited for people who can self-insure.

Are there myths or misconceptions that prevent people from getting their finances in order?

Teresa Yent: As we age, I believe we get more set in our ways and how we think. We have clients who think, "As long as the Republicans are in charge, life will be good," and vice versa with the Democrats. The truth is, it doesn't really matter. The stock market does what it does, and it doesn't depend on what is happening in Washington as much as people think. The president can't change things as readily as people think he can.

How has the recent pandemic impacted the financial services industry?

Teresa Yent: I feel sorry for our clients who retired in 2018 or 2019 because now they're here in the height of their go-go years, and they can't go. It's been very frustrating for them. They had all these items on their bucket lists and traveling they wanted to do, and they couldn't do any of it because of COVID. The older you are, the more afraid you are of the different variants of COVID going around. They're stuck at home, and many of our clients choose to turn off their income. We have them set up on what we call a "paycheck," which shows up automatically in their checking account each month. They said, "Stop. We aren't spending it. We aren't going anywhere, doing anything, or going out to eat." Everything kind of went on pause for them for a while.

As for strategies, we're very unconstrained with the way we manage money. We will go all to cash if we need to. We did that in 2008 when the writing was on the wall pretty early. We started being defensive back in February and March of 2020. We used a variety of buffered products, which constrained the amounts of loss and gain any given account could have. It offered them a smoother ride, which most people look for in retirement. Once people stop working and getting that regular paycheck from employment, they get more conservative with their investments.

Teresa, what inspired you to get started in the financial services field?

Teresa Yent: I originally got started back in the 90s. I was looking for something I could do that gave me some flexibility. I had children at home, but I wanted to work while they were in school all day long. Every time I described the job I desired, my husband would say, "It sounds like you want to do insurance," although I wasn't entirely sure I wanted to do insurance. My uncle was in the insurance business and inspired me to pursue this career. I ended up working in the senior market with Medicare supplements, long-term care insurance, and simple fixed annuities. I called on people who were retired and at home during the day, and it was extremely rewarding. I enjoyed working with them. This career gave me the flexibility to be with my kids when I needed to and work more when I wanted to.

My husband was a road warrior and traveled worldwide, and his kidneys died. He went on dialysis and went on Social Security Disability while waiting for a kidney transplant. We got some very poor advice and bad strategies regarding tax and social security. We always said that if we could figure it out, we'd love to help other people. Once he got his kidney and had a new lease on life, my husband joined my business and started doing more of the retirement planning. He previously worked in the IT world within the securities business, and he always wanted to have a securities license. He went and obtained several securities licenses and dragged me, kicking and screaming to get mine. It was one of the best decisions I have ever made. We work together every day, love being together, and love helping people. We absolutely love our clients and have beautiful, personal relationships with each and every one of them.

How can people find you, connect with you, and learn more?

Teresa Yent: The name of our business is Golden Years Advisors. Our website is www.goldenyearsadvisors.com. You can reach us by phone at 919-755-4889. We are in the beautiful city of Raleigh, North Carolina, but we have clients all over the country.

Jim and Teresa Yent are Investment Advisor Representatives of and securities are offered through USA Financial Securities, 6020 E. Fulton St., Ada, MI 49301. Member FINRA/SIPC. A Registered Investment Advisor. Golden Years Advisors is not affiliated with USA Financial Securities

TERESA YENT, ChFC, CLTC

Founder

Golden Years Advisors

Teresa's career started in 1997 in insurance that included Medicare Supplements, Long Term Care, and Fixed Annuities. Her husband, Jim, joined her business in 2002 with wealth management and retirement planning. Teresa became a financial advisor earning her ChFC and CLTC and loves their focus on comprehensive retirement planning. It is important for Teresa to be an independent financial professional, allowing her the freedom to find the best solution for clients. Teresa has many passions in her life. Working with the love of her life daily is the best!

PHONE: 919-755-4889

WEBSITE: https://www.goldenyearsadvisors.com/

EMAIL: Teresa@goldenyearsadvisors.com

FACEBOOK: https://www.facebook.com/goldenyearsadvisors/

NATHAN
BRINKMAN

NATHAN BRINKMAN

Conversation with Nathan Brinkman

Nathan, you are the founder of Triumph Wealth Management. Tell us about your work and the people you help.

Nathan Brinkman: We work with people who own and run companies and are typically at that intersection of transition and succession of their businesses. We're celebrating our 15th year in business. I've been doing this for over 27 years. I decided to grow up and listen to the experts in our industry that said, "If you have the courage, be really good at one or two things, versus trying to be really good at everything else." And so that's what I did 15 years ago. I created a firm specifically designed to help business owners from the corporate and business perspective and an individual perspective.

What specific concerns and challenges do business owners have?

Nathan Brinkman: Well, you know, that's a fascinating study right there. Many business owners don't even know they're in that mode. I always joke about getting that call on a Friday afternoon from an owner saying, "I'm going to make an offer on a house down in Florida over the weekend. And I want out of my business on Monday morning." I say that a bit facetiously, but not really. Business owners have the entrepreneurial gene in their bodies, and they move fast. All of the businesses we work with are successful, mature businesses. And many of them have developed a wealth point where they want to know the next step. And yet they've been so cemented in their business it's hard for them to think outside of it. Typically, we work with people who have curious minds and wonder what they should be doing. Many feel like they should become experts on their own. But they quickly realize it is a very sophisticated game, dealing with tax impact and personal lives. For instance, they wonder if they need to go home and get a permission slip from their spouse to retire because they have become accustomed to a particular lifestyle. So it's a really sticky intersection.

When we first meet a client, we ask, "What drives and motivates you? Why are you at this intersection?" Sometimes it is raw success, and they think they have enough, but they need someone else to tell them they have enough. Sometimes it's frustration. We feel that right now in today's "Great

Resignation." It's challenging to satisfy people, keep a culture going, work with people remotely, recruit, and retain folks. It becomes exhausting. And I see the burnout right now. So many people are reaching out to us for those reasons.

Selling your business is an incredibly private topic. We used to host seminars, and we found out that even people who really wanted to come wouldn't show up. They didn't want other people in a public setting to know they were thinking about selling their business. It's really taboo.

The last thing we help business owners do is to identify the worth of their assets. Often their net worth is tied back to the business. And yet they really don't know what it's worth. So we spend a great deal of time ensuring they understand the quality and the amount of the assets and how that should transfer through. Sometimes that's good news, and sometimes it's bad news. So we spend a lot of time identifying the core key things they should consider because they don't even know where to start. Then we dig down to the number one question of, "What the heck is this thing worth?"

Has the "Great Resignation" caused you to see an uptick of people wanting to sell their businesses?

Nathan Brinkman: Absolutely. We're at an intersection of a lot of money chasing a few goods. So there is this fear of going to market. Private equity is very active, and we see it coming down to $5 million or $10 million businesses. Before, those were $50 million or $100 million businesses. There is excellent activity out there; lots of cash chasing a few companies. Then we also have this "Silver Tsunami" happening. If you look at the demographics, many of these companies are owned by people with a little bit of silver in their hair. Sometimes they hit the selling intersection, and impulsivity strikes. We know that many people who sell their businesses regret the transaction afterward. A lot of it is because they rushed into it and didn't equip themselves appropriately. Many people who buy businesses professionally know precisely how to get owners to feel like they need to do the deal now, or it's not going to happen. But we're like, "Whoa, whoa whoa. Trust me; if you've got a good solid business and a buyer wants it, they will be willing to wait a couple of months. You have to get yourself prepared."

Especially today, if an owner has been on the fence about selling, there is no better time with so many buyers in the market. Buyers and money - it's a dangerous combination. We're seeing crazy numbers in terms of what sellers are getting, which is great. So if you are in selling mode, it's an excellent time. It isn't much different than the real estate market. For example, my wife and I have a really nice house, and I love it. But I'd also love it if someone else bought it for what I think it's worth, and I could go do something different. But my wife doesn't want to sell. And you know what they say, "Happy wife, happy life." So we're not interested in selling because what she wants is important to me. I see that a lot in the business world too. The hesitation isn't about whether or not there is activity in the market; it is about getting everyone on the same page about the transaction.

Are there myths and misconceptions owners have about selling their businesses?

Nathan Brinkman: I always liken it to the country club conversation, right? So it's in the paper, the news, or the business reg that "so and so sold their business." And suppose I'm at the country club, and I sell my business for $50 million. In that case, I don't necessarily want everybody to know that. But just because that's the sale price, that doesn't mean it's what I received, right? So there are a lot of things that happen behind closed doors. Very often, we see a guy out on the golf course saying to his buddy, "I heard you sold your business for $50 million." And the guy automatically thinks *his* business must be worth $50 million. The point is; no two deals are identical. Many formulas, factors, and complexities go into the process. In my experience, owners who arm themselves with the appropriate information generally work out the best deals with the least amount of regret. You absolutely should surround yourself with experienced professionals who can guide you through the process.

I'm one of those guys who is straightforward. So I'll tell you if it's good or bad. I don't have a horse in the race, especially in the beginning. Some people will appreciate that, many won't, and that's fine. But if you look at a team of professionals involved in the deal, many of them are paid at a successful conclusion. And therefore, once something gets rolling, there tends to be a lot of favoritism towards "let's get this thing done." I want to say that we're more of that planning and pragmatic side. We're running the math and making sure the deal works for the business *and* the individual. At the end of the day, these are closely held companies we work with, and the consequences can be incredibly devastating. Rational thought is one of the first things that goes out the door in high emotion situations. We like to help people align goals, dreams, and priorities to get back to that rational thought process. There are better results and less regret when you're in a rational thought process.

Nathan, what inspired you to get started in this industry?

Nathan Brinkman: Well, I like to say I have this mental illness sickness known as, "I grew up in it." I grew up in a small town in South Dakota, and my parents owned the office product store on Main Street in the 1980s. Everything was going great until my dad expanded the business at exactly the wrong time. And so the friendly bankers who were encouraging all of this growth quickly became the friendly bankers who were reaching inside of his till every day. My dad was forced to sell out of that business, to make a long story short. He had a passion for technology, specifically computers. He was a serial entrepreneur. My grandfather was an entrepreneur, and my other grandfather on my mom's side was a farmer. So I have always been surrounded by these people that run their own things and are used to taking a lot of risks. It became very natural for me. As I got into the professional space, I found that I knew the language of people that run their own businesses.

For the first half of my career, I focused on helping people post-transaction, investing the money, doing the estate planning strategies, tax planning, all that kind of stuff. And I realized that if I got involved way earlier, maybe I could change some of the mistakes that happened in my own family. And that's really what drives and motivates me today; it's incredibly personal. I'm passionate about it, just because I felt the effects as a young man having deals that didn't go well. And I know that this kind of counsel and advice results in a lot of positivity for people. It is not the most profitable side of wealth management practice to be early in the deal. But again, if we do it for the right reasons, our firm does incredibly well. I like to be involved way early in the process. And again, for me, as I had that entrepreneurial spirit, I wanted to be involved because I liked the outcome. One of the best ways I get paid is when my clients are so thankful for a good deal. My head hits the pillow, and I sleep well, knowing I help people in that capacity.

What should people consider when choosing who to work with?

Nathan Brinkman: I think you have to work with a team of professionals. People often go back to who they feel most comfortable with, such as their accountant, banker, or attorney. But they kind of forget about other professionals that need to be involved. Not to pick on other professionals, but they may not have the same experience. I mean that many CPAs and attorneys don't own a firm. There is a disconnect when it comes to dealing with business owners who are key decision-makers. So it's essential to surround yourself with a team of professionals, making sure somebody acts as a quarterback, gathering all the information, and keeping everybody abreast along the way. That's what we do. We have a systematic process, and you should clearly see it. You should see the steps of how this thing will go, and you should see integration with other professionals. If you have somebody that wants to control it from beginning to end, it typically doesn't end well. I appreciate why other professionals want to control the whole thing. But steps tend to get missed, whether it's a tax or legal impact. That is what separates us in the industry. We have a tenured, disciplined process we walk through in the beginning. We do a lot of planning on the front end to identify the objectives and goals so that everybody on the planning team is aware. Once we do that, we set the strategy, which is the most important thing, and we decide where we want the accountant, the attorney, the bank, and the business. We want everybody involved because we know the more heads working on the same set of data, the better. When you have disconnected data, it's challenging. It may become expensive because every other professional wants to bill to catch up.

How do people find you, connect with you, and learn more?

Nathan Brinkman: You can find me on LinkedIn at Triumph Wealth. Our website is www.triumphwealth.com, and my email address is nathan@triumphwealth.com. Most people schedule via our website through Calendly to connect with us for 15 minutes. I'm happy to help.

NATHAN BRINKMAN

President, CEO, & Founder

Triumph Wealth Management

Growing up in a family business in South Dakota created lifelong memories for me. I understand the ups and downs of owning a business and all it entails, as I am a business owner as well.

I am a Certified Family Business Specialist and work with business owners, executives, and their families to ensure the necessary strategies are in place to help secure their financial future.

Helping high net worth clients identify and analyze challenges and opportunities, I am also a Certified Private Wealth Advisor® and Certified Exit Planning Advisor. The Certified Private Wealth Advisor® (CPWA®) certification program is an advanced credential for wealth managers who work with high net worth individuals, focusing on life cycle of wealth: accumulation, preservation, and distribution. The program focused on behavioral finance, charitable and estate planning, planning for closely-held business owners, planning for executives, portfolio management, retirement planning, risk management, and tax planning.

Many business owners find that their personal and business lives are practically inseparable. I feel this demonstrates the importance of financial planning, which takes into account the unique considerations and opportunities of owning and operating a business.

Having been in the financial services industry since 1995, I have worked with numerous business owners and executive management to identify, anticipate and avoid the most common mistakes that plague businesses. This includes addressing the financial needs and products for every stage of a business life cycle while taking into account personal financial goals and dreams.

My wife and I reside in Madison, Wisconsin, with our three children. In my free time, I enjoy spending time with my family and traveling. I also have a passion for BBQ. I am a member of the Wisconsin Family Business Center and WTBA (Wisconsin Transportation Builders Association).

EMAIL: nathan@triumphwealth.com

WEBSITE: www.triumphwealth.com

PHONE: 608-828-4400

ABOUT THE PUBLISHER

Mark Imperial is a Best-Selling Author, Syndicated Business Columnist, Syndicated Radio Host, and internationally recognized Stage, Screen, and Radio Host of numerous business shows spotlighting leading experts, entrepreneurs, and business celebrities.

His passion is to discover noteworthy business owners, professionals, experts, and leaders who do great work and share their stories and secrets to their success with the world on his syndicated radio program titled "Remarkable Radio."

Mark is also the media marketing strategist and voice for some of the world's most famous brands. You can hear his voice over the airwaves weekly on Chicago radio and world-wide on iHeart Radio.

Mark is a Karate black belt; teaches Muay Thai and Kickboxing; loves Thai food, House Music, and his favorite TV shows are infomercials.

Learn more:

www.MarkImperial.com
www.BooksGrowBusiness.com